GENTLE
MANATEES

by Kathleen Martin-James

Lerner Publications Company • Minneapolis

The manatee is an amazing animal. Sadly, like so many other amazing animals on our planet, manatees are endangered because of humans. I hope that by learning about animals, children will grow to care for them and to make choices that will help protect them. This book is for Aidan.

This book is available in two editions:
Library binding by Lerner Publications Company, a division of Lerner Publishing Group, Inc.
Soft cover by First Avenue Editions, an imprint of Lerner Publishing Group, Inc.
241 First Avenue North
Minneapolis, MN 55401 U.S.A.

Website address: www.lernerbooks.com

Words in *italic* type are explained in a glossary on page 30.

Library of Congress Cataloging-in-Publication Data

Martin-James, Kathleen.
    Gentle manatees / by Kathleen Martin-James.
       p.   cm. — (Pull ahead books)
    Includes index.
    ISBN-13: 978-0-8225-2422-9 (lib. bdg. : alk. paper)
    ISBN-10: 0-8225-2422-8 (lib. bdg. : alk. paper)
    ISBN-13: 978-0-8225-2441-0 (pbk. : alk. paper)
    ISBN-10: 0-8225-2441-4 (pbk. : alk. paper)
    1. West Indian manatee—Juvenile literature. I. Title.
    II. Series.
QL737.S63M365 2005
599.55—dc22   2004017914

Manufactured in the United States of America
4 – CG – 4/1/13

This roly-poly animal is a manatee.
It is shaped like a giant potato.

A manatee has wrinkly skin
that is grayish brown.

Sometimes tiny green plants
called *algae* grow on its skin.

A manatee has small eyes and a *snout*. A manatee's nose and mouth are part of its snout.

How big do you think a manatee is?

An adult manatee is as long as
two bathtubs. It can weigh
as much as a cow.

Where do manatees live?

Sometimes manatees live in salty water. The ocean has salty water.

Sometimes they live in freshwater. Freshwater is water that is not salty.

Manatees cannot live in cold water or very deep water.

They must stay in warm,
shallow water where plants grow.

Manatees eat plants. Animals
that eat only plants are called
herbivores.

A manatee uses its front flippers to help it eat.

What else does it use its flippers for?

This manatee is using its flippers to move along the floor of the ocean.

A manatee moves its wide, flat tail up and down to help it swim.

Manatees can eat and swim underwater. But they cannot breathe underwater.

How do manatees breathe?

A manatee floats to the top of the water. It pokes the tip of its snout into the air and breathes in.

Then it goes back underwater.

Can you see the hair
on this manatee's snout?

Manatees are *mammals*.
Mammals have hair on their bodies.

Baby mammals *nurse*.
They drink their mother's milk.

A baby manatee is called a *calf*.

A mother manatee teaches her calf where to find warm water and which plants to eat.

A calf stays
close to its
mother.

Squeak! The calf makes noises
so its mother knows where it is.

The calf will stay near its mother for two years.

Then it will live on its own.

Adult manatees spend a lot of time swimming alone.

They are curious and go exploring.

In the winter, manatees swim to places where the water is warm.

Manatees play when
they are together.

Sometimes
they even
hug.

Manatees are gentle.
They don't hurt other animals.

And other animals rarely hurt manatees.

Many people study manatees.

They want to help manatees
stay safe.

Then manatees can keep swimming, exploring, and playing in the water.

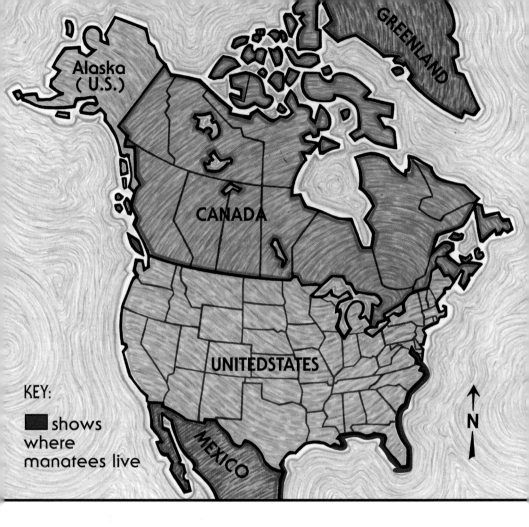

KEY:

■ shows where manatees live

Find your state or province on this map.
Do manatees live near you?

Parts of a Manatee's Body

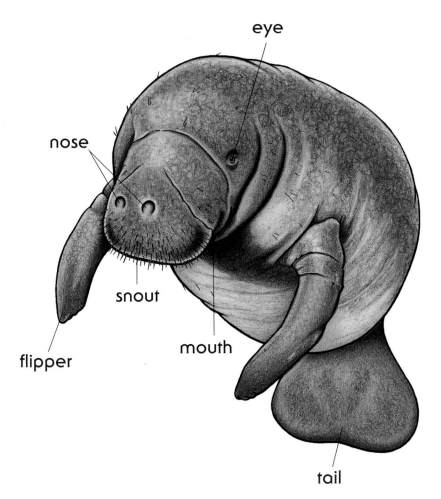

eye

nose

snout

flipper

mouth

tail

Glossary

algae: tiny green plants

calf: a baby manatee

herbivores: animals that eat only plants

mammals: animals that drink their mother's milk while they are young. Mammals also breathe air and have hair on their bodies.

nurse: to drink mother's milk

shallow: not deep

snout: the part of an animal's head that includes its nose, mouth, and jaws

Index

About the Author

Kathleen Martin-James was born in Toronto, Ontario. She has lived in many different places across Canada and in the United States. Now she lives in Halifax, Nova Scotia, with her husband, Mike, and their little son, Aidan. Kathleen loves to read and to write. She also enjoys working with Mike and fishermen across Atlantic Canada to help save the leatherback sea turtle, her favorite animal. Like the manatee, the leatherback turtle is an endangered species.

Textual Note: The West Indian manatee, the species that includes the Florida manatee, is endangered. As with any endangered species, the reasons behind its decline are complicated. The current major threats to its survival are habitat destruction and injuries from boat propellers.

Photo Acknowledgments

The photographs in this book are reproduced through the courtesy of: © Tom and Therisa Stack/TOM STACK & ASSOCIATES, INC., front cover, p. 3; © Brian Parker/TOM STACK AND ASSOCIATES, INC., pp. 4, 6, 7, 11, 16; © James Watt/Visuals Unlimited, p. 5; © Doug Perrine/SeaPics.com, pp. 8, 12, 19, 20, 21, 22, 24, 25, 31; © Jeff Foott/TOM STACK AND ASSOCIATES, INC., pp. 9, 10, 18; © Brandon Cole/Visuals Unlimited, pp. 13, 26, 27; © Tom Stack/TOM STACK AND ASSOCIATES, INC., p. 14; © Marty Snyderman/Visuals Unlimited, pp. 15, 17; © Tom Campbell/SeaPics.com, p. 23.